# MEMOIR

OF THE

# HON. ABBOTT LAWRENCE,

PREPARED FOR THE

MASSACHUSETTS HISTORICAL SOCIETY,

BY

HON. NATHAN APPLETON.

---

BOSTON:
1856.
J. H. EASTBURN'S PRESS.

In the interest of creating a more extensive selection of rare historical book reprints, we have chosen to reproduce this title even though it may possibly have occasional imperfections such as missing and blurred pages, missing text, poor pictures, markings, dark backgrounds and other reproduction issues beyond our control. Because this work is culturally important, we have made it available as a part of our commitment to protecting, preserving and promoting the world's literature. Thank you for your understanding.

# MEMOIR.

The duty of preparing a memoir of ABBOTT LAWRENCE for the Massachusetts Historical Society, agreeably to their appointment, is undertaken as a sad, but pleasing labor of love, by one who, during a large part of his life, was not only engaged in similar pursuits, but was on terms of the greatest personal intimacy with him.

Mr. Lawrence was by profession a merchant—a profession which is not often associated with the higher exhibitions of intellect. It is true it is often accompanied with great wealth, and wealth alone carries with it power, and a certain degree of distinction.

The merchant is at the head of the numerous family who live by trade—in the distribution, on a smaller or larger scale, of the commodities which supply the wants and fancies of life. The whole family is actuated immediately and directly by the selfish principle, in its application to property. The sole object of trade is profit—gain to the trader. Other occupations and professions, whilst tied down by the common necessity of providing for the wants of life, are associated with other aims which command the higher places in the world's estimation.

Notwithstanding the eloquent expostulations of the friends of peace, the world continues to assign the foremost rank to the successful warrior, who fights for glory as well as patriotism. A Napoleon or a Wellington always commands the applause of his day and generation. Even Washington won his glory as a warrior before he was known as the statesman. In the learned professions—in the various departments of science—and in the higher walks of art, it is the love of fame which is the spur to excellence, rather than any pecuniary acquisition. The same principle will apply, in a considerable degree, to the mechanic arts. It is true that some modification of the selfish principle may be said to lie at the root of all human action, but nowhere is it so naked and undisguised as in the profession of the merchant, whose direct and avowed object is the getting of gain. At the same time, the world has always given honor to merchants. We are told in Holy Writ, that "the traffickers of Tyre were the honorable of the Earth," and the same character has been freely bestowed in all succeeding ages. It is to be taken for granted, however, that it has always been the use made of the wealth acquired in trade, which has been the object of commendation and honor, rather than the success in its accumulation.

The merchant makes no claim to benevolence or patriotism as his ruling motive in trade: all he professes is absolute and undeviating justice. The morals of trade are of the strictest and purest character. It is not an uncommon opinion that there is a laxity in the mercantile code, which looks with indulgence on what are called the tricks of trade. It is not so. Whilst the direct object of all trade is gain, individual benefit, not the slightest prevarication or deviation from truth is allowable. There is no class of men with whom the Christian rule of doing to others what we expect or require in return, is more strictly demanded, than amongst merchants. Mercantile honor is as delicate and fragile as that of a woman. It will not bear the slightest stain. The man in trade who has been found to equivocate or falter in his course, becomes a marked man. He is avoided. It is thus found, by experience, that integrity is almost as uniformly the accompaniment of success, as it always is of character. It is true, that in the manifold operations of trade, there are opportunities and temptations to acts of dishonesty, more frequent than in other occupations, and it is not to be denied that, in many instances, poor human nature is found to yield to them. What we insist on is the rigidity of the rule which controls the action of the honorable merchant, and under which alone he can claim that name.

But whilst the selfish principle lies at the foundation of trade, there is no reason why the trader himself should not be active in benevolence and all the Christian virtues. There is no occupation which has a tendency to liberalize the mind more than that of the merchant. His intercourse is wide with men of all opinions and of all countries. He perceives that integrity, virtue, and honor, are not confined to a narrow circle, or to one country. We accordingly find a full proportion of men engaged in trade among the patrons and managers of our charitable and benevolent institutions. They are also amongst the most liberal supporters of enterprises undertaken for the public good. It is perhaps natural that men accumulating their own fortunes, should have less hesitation in adventuring property in new enterprises, than those holding property by inheritance. The fact appears to be so. These general views of the mercantile profession may serve as an appropriate introduction to the life of one who was so eminent an ornament of that profession, and whose whole career was an illustration of the integrity, liberality, and public spirit, which are indispensable elements in the character of the great and good merchant.

ABBOTT LAWRENCE was born in the town of Groton, Massachusetts, December 16th, 1792. He was the fifth son of Deacon Samuel Lawrence, a respectable farmer, who did good service as a soldier during the revolutionary war, in which he rose to the rank of major, and was highly esteemed by his fellow-citizens. The ancestor, John Lawrence, one of the early Puritan emigrants, settled at Watertown in 1635, and removed to Groton in 1660. He came from Wissett, in Suffolk, where, and in the neighboring parish of Rumburg, the family had been long settled. It was of great antiquity, Sir Robert Lawrence having been knighted by Richard Cœur de Lion, in 1191, for his bravery in scaling the walls of Acre. The early education of the subject of this memoir was at the district school during the winter, and for a few months at the Academy which now bears his name. This was the narrow foundation on which he himself added the superstructure which has carried him successfully through the various places which he was destined to fill. With this, the common outfit of every New England boy, he came to Boston, in 1808, as an apprentice to his brother Amos, who was already established in business, and who thus speaks of him in his diary: "In 1808 he came to me, as my apprentice, bringing his bundle under his arm, with less than three dollars in his pocket, and this was his fortune. A first-rate business lad he was, but, like other bright lads, needed the careful eye of a senior to guard him from the pit-falls that he was exposed to." He is reported to have been most assiduous and diligent in his duties, and to have devoted his evenings to supply the deficiencies of his early education. The business of the elder brother was prosperous, and when Abbott came of age, in 1814, a copartnership was formed between them, which continued until terminated by death. Their business was the importation and sale of foreign manufactures, in which the firm stood at the head of that class of merchants— and by their industry and enterprise acquired a large fortune. Under the tariffs of 1816 and 1824 the manufacture of cottons and woollens was extensively introduced, and the house of A. & A. Lawrence entered largely into their sales on commission. It was not until the year 1830 that they became interested in the cotton mills at Lowell.

On the establishment of the Suffolk, Tremont, and Lawrence Companies, as well as subsequently in other corporations, they became large proprietors. From this time, their business, as selling agents, was on the most extensive scale, and their income from all sources large in proportion. As a man of business, Mr. Lawrence possessed talents of the very first order. Prompt, energetic, with an intuitive insight into the characters of men, with sound judgment and an openness of character which won favor on the slightest acquaintance, he acquired the confidence of the community in the highest degree. For many of the last years of his life, he was largely interested in the China trade, the source of a good deal of profit. But his mind was not confined to the numerous details and ramifications of his business, extensive as it was. He took a deep interest in all matters of public concern, in politics, political economy, finance. He was amongst the most zealous advocates of the protective system, before he was himself interested in manufactures, and was one of the delegates from Massachusetts to Harrisburg, in 1827, where he took an active part in the deliberations of that assembly. In 1834, he was elected a member of the twenty-fourth Congress, for the district of Suffolk. He was placed at once on the Committee of Ways and Means, where his acquaintance with mercantile affairs gave him much deserved influence. He won the favor of all parties, by his general intelligence, and by his genial and affable manners. Without making set speeches for display, he spoke well, on proper occasions, on the matters of business before Congress. He declined a re-election at the end of the term, but in 1839, in consequence of a vacancy, he was with difficulty persuaded to allow himself to be a candidate for the twenty-sixth Congress, to which he was triumphantly elected. His usefulness in this position was, however, soon brought to a close, by a severe attack of fever, in March, 1840, on his recovery from which, he considered it necessary to resign the office.

In 1842, he was appointed, on the part of Massachusetts, a Commissioner on the subject of the Northeastern Boundary, which had become a most dangerous and difficult question, entrusted on the part of the British government to Lord Ashburton. It is the belief of the writer, who was then in Congress and in daily confidential communication with him, that to Mr. Lawrence, more than to any other individual, is due the successful accomplishment of the negotiation, which resulted in the important treaty of Washington. Lord Ashburton was himself a merchant, of an open, straight-forward character. He had accepted the office of Ambassador with the especial purpose of settling this vexed question. Mr. Lawrence accepted the office of Commissioner with much the same feeling. They were both of opinion that any terms of settlement which involved no sacrifice of honor, were better than that this portentous question should remain unsettled, liable at any moment to break out into a regular war.

They soon came to an understanding with each other. Lord Ashburton communicated freely to Mr. Lawrence the utmost limits to which his instructions would allow him to go, and Mr. Lawrence was thus enabled to bring his somewhat intractable colleagues to the final happy issue. He was at last, at the close of the negotiation, called in to satisfy the scruples of President Tyler, who had found a difficulty in his own mind with some of the details, which Mr. Webster, the Secretary of State, was unable to remove.

In the Presidential campaign of 1840, he took an active part in favor of the election of Gen. Harrison. In September, 1842, he was President of the Whig Convention, which nominated Henry Clay for President, on the part of Massachusetts. He was a delegate to the Whig National Convention in 1844, and, in the same year, one of the electors at large for the State. In the Presidential canvass of 1848, the name of Mr. Lawrence was prominently associated for the office of Vice-President with that of Gen. Taylor for President, and at the convention in Philadelphia he wanted but six votes of being nominated for that office. This result was owing to the peculiar and unexpected course of some of the delegates of his own State. He was disappointed, but never allowed his equanimity to be disturbed. He had, with extreme delicacy, forborne to allow his name to be brought forward by his friends until the last moment, and he did not allow any personal feeling to affect his course. He presided at a ratification meeting, in Faneuil Hall, to sustain the nomination of Taylor and Fillmore. As a presiding officer, on this and similar occasions, he appeared to great advantage. He was, in fact, a self-made, but very successful and forcible public speaker. This was shown effectively, during this campaign, in what are called caucus speeches, in which he was always happy. He was urgently solicited, in various quarters of the country, to address his fellow-citizens, but confined himself to a few of the most important points, in which he was eminently successful.

Immediately after the inauguration of Gen. Taylor, he was summoned to Washington, and urged to take a seat in the Cabinet. But the two highest places had been disposed of, and those which remained were not to his taste, and were declined. A higher position was soon after offered him,—that of the Representative of the United States at the Court of Great Britain. This is a station of the highest honor, which has been filled by some of the most eminent men of the country, requiring sound discretion as the necessary foundation, and in which the highest and the most varied information upon all subjects will find full exercise. This place, after some hesitation, he accepted, and, with Mrs. Lawrence, embarked for England in September, 1849. It is difficult to find greater contrasts in the life of any man, than those presented by his first and last visits to England—the first as a novice, confined to the operations of trade at Manchester and Leeds, and the last introducing him directly to Queen Victoria and the British Court, and giving him free intercourse with the most distinguished Statesmen of the land. This position he occupied not merely respectably, but with the highest honor, not only to himself, but to his country. He did not attempt to pass for what he was not, but his general information, especially upon matters relating to trade, commerce, and finance, caused his opinions to be sought in the highest quarters, whilst his peculiar urbanity and gracious manners made him a favorite with all with whom he came in contact. The possession of an ample fortune enabled him to support a style of hospitality more in accordance with the higher European embassies, than is usual under the somewhat niggardly allowance of our own government. All this, however, he did without overstepping the bounds of the strictest propriety and decorum. On public occasions, and at the numerous festivals which he attended, he acquitted himself in the happiest manner,—and his speeches may well cômpare with those made by Statesmen of the highest education.

Having had an opportunity of examining copies of his diplomatic correspondence, a small portion only of which has been published, the writer has no hesitation in characterising it as exceedingly able, both in matter and manner, and as comparing well with the best specimens of that species of composition. It is very evident that he inspired the deepest respect in the different functionaries with whom he came in contact.

One of the first objects requiring his attention, was the project of a ship canal from the Caribbean Sea to the Pacific Ocean, which had been brought forward by his predecessor, Mr. Bancroft. The assent and guarantee of both the United States and Great Britain were necessary to effect this object. An obstacle existed in the claim set up by Great Britain to the Protectorate of the Mosquito Territory, on a part of which the eastern terminus of the canal must be made. This subject was one which received his immediate attention, and, as early as December, 1849, he obtained from Lord Palmerston a disavowal, on the part of Great Britain, of any intention "to occupy or colonize Nicaragua, Costa Rica, the Mosquito Coast, or any part of Central America." His mind was very much occupied with this matter, in the expectation that it would devolve on him to negotiate a treaty with the British Government. In a letter of December 14th, 1849, to Lord Palmerston, he presents a view of the important advantages to result from such a canal, and of the obstacle interposed by the claim in behalf of the Mosquito Indians as an Independent Sovereignty. In the mean time, he set himself to work in collecting information in illustration of the connection of the British Government with the Mosquito Indians, out of which their claim to certain peculiar rights as their protectors was founded. In this, he was entirely successful. He became possessed of some very important manuscript documents, which had never been published, consisting of the Vernon and Wager manuscripts, which he characterizes as "A collection embodying, in the original, official as well as private letters of the Duke of Newcastle, of Sir Charles Wager, of Admiral Vernon, of Sir William

Pulteney, of Governor Trelawney, of Mr. Robert Hodgson and many others, a mass of authentic information never published, and not existing anywhere else, unless in Her Majesty's State Paper Office."

He was arranging all these matters into a legal argument and historical document, when in April, 1850, he received notice from Mr. Clayton, Secretary of State, that "these negotiations were entirely transferred to Washington, and that he was to cease altogether to press them in London." This was naturally a severe disappointment, but he at once set about changing the character of this document from a letter to Lord Palmerston, to a despatch to our own Secretary of State. It bears date 19th April, 1850. It covers eighty-five folio pages of manuscript. It discusses the question of the title of the Mosquito Indians to the sovereignty of the country claimed for them by Great Britain. It states, very clearly, the law established by the different nations of Europe, in reference to their own rights, and that of the Savages inhabiting the continent and islands of America. "The Christian world have agreed in recognizing the Indians as occupants only of the lands, without a right of possession, without domain, the sovereignty being determined by priority of discovery, and occupation."

In the historical review of the question, he states that Spain established her rights on the Mosquito territory in the 15th century, which were recognized in the treaty of 1672 by Sir William Godolphin. He quotes from the documents beforementioned, abundant evidence of the tampering of the Governor of Jamaica, and of the Admiral on that station, with the Mosquitoes, during the war which broke out with Spain in 1739. The treaty of 1763, as well as that of 1783, would seem to admit the sovereignty of Spain in the fullest degree. This whole question is argued with great ability. It is unfortunate that whilst this document was on its passage to Washington, a treaty was actually signed by Mr. Clayton and Sir Henry L. Bulwer, out of which a serious misunderstanding has arisen. This could hardly have happened, had this document been communicated to the British government, as the American view of the question.

Mr. Lawrence's own view of the subject was, "that whenever the history of the conduct of Great Britain shall be published to the world, it will not stand one hour before the bar of public opinion without universal condemnation." *

A question was left unsettled by Mr. Bancroft, in relation to the postal rates on the transit of letters across England, to which Mr. Lawrence devoted a good deal of time. Not being able to induce the Postmaster-General to adopt rates more reasonable than the existing ones, he recommended to our government to give notice to annul the convention of 1848, as they had a right to do, as the only means of bringing about a more equitable arrangement.

Another matter which Mr. Lawrence pressed upon the British Government with earnestness and ability,

---

* This document was published on a call from the Senate, February 9th, 1853. Senate Doc. 82d Congress, 2d session, No. 27.

was the injustice of her light-house system, by which foreign tonnage is taxed to support sinecure offices, whilst our own light-houses are free to all the world, without any tax whatever. These despatches, which were never satisfactorily answered, were made public by vote of the House of Commons on motion of Mr. Hume.

A delicate but spirited correspondence took place between Mr. Lawrence and Lord Granville in relation to the outrage committed by H. M. ship Express on the steamer Prometheus, for which an ample apology was made.

In August, 1852, England was thrown into intense excitement, in consequence of a letter written by Mr. Webster on the subject of the new ground taken by Great Britain in reference to the fisheries. This led to several interviews between Mr. Lawrence and Lord Malmesbury, the result of which was such a modification of the instructions to the vessels on the station as prevented any collision. His attention was unremitted in reference to the very numerous private claims upon the British Government which required his care. A joint commission was afterward appointed to decide definitively upon this description of cases.

In September, 1851, Mr. and Mrs. Lawrence made a tour in Ireland, of which he gives an interesting account in a despatch under date of 2d December. They visited Dublin, Galway, Limerick, Killarney, Cork, &c. In many of these places, he was met by deputations, and received the most flattering and respectful attentions. His account of the present state of Ireland, and his remarks upon it are in the highest degree interesting and instructive.

On the whole it may be doubted whether, since the mission of Dr. Franklin, any minister of the United States has accomplished a diplomatic success greater than must be awarded to Mr. Lawrence. This was the result of his peculiar endowments, quick apprehension, sagacity, retentive memory, power of reaching the pith of a matter, tact, kindness of heart, and perfect truthfulness.

His residence in London, mingling freely in society, did much in producing a change in public opinion, favorable to his own country. The writer thought he saw good evidence of this at a dinner at which he was present, given by Mr. Westhead, member of Parliament for Knaresborough, at the Clarendon Hotel, to a party of about fifty, consisting equally of English and Americans. This gentleman had met Mr. Lawrence during a visit which he made to Manchester and Liverpool, and was so much pleased with him that he requested permission to give him such a dinner, which it would have been ungracious to refuse. It was a compliment to Mr. Lawrence and his country, graced by the presence of distinguished members of the British Cabinet, and such Americans as happened to be in England. It was opened by a neat speech from Mr. Westhead, to which Mr. Lawrence replied in his happiest manner. Speeches followed by Lord Palmerston, Mr. Gladstone, Earl Powis, Mr. Cardwell, and others. They were beautiful specimens of dinner speeches; but what was particularly striking, was the amiable manner in which they tendered the right hand of fellowship to their American brothers. There seemed to be a general desire to express the feeling that brother Jonathan had proved himself a worthy chip of the old block, and was entitled to their kindest regards. There was an air of sincerity and cordiality on the occasion which could not be mistaken. Unfortunately, reporters were excluded, so that these speeches were never given to the public.

After three years' service, Mr. Lawrence obtained leave to return to his country, which he did in October, 1852. On this occasion, he was invited to a public dinner, but happening at a period when the whole community were deeply affected by the recent death of Mr. Webster, he declined it;—he arrived, in fact, barely in time to attend the funeral of that lamented statesman.

Mr. Lawrence was always ready and foremost in supporting measures which promised benefit to the public. He was a large subscriber to the various railroads projected for the concentration of trade in Boston, and this from a feeling of patriotism, rather than the expectation of profit. His subscriptions for public objects of charity or education were always on the most liberal scale; but the crowning act of this character was the establishment of the Scientific School at Cambridge, connected with Harvard College, for which he gave fifty thousand dollars in 1847, and left a further like sum by his will. His letter to Mr. Eliot, the treasurer of the College, accompanying the donation, was a proof how completely his mind was imbued with the subject, and how fully and accurately he had investigated it. This institution supplied a great want in our system of education, in the application of science to the arts. He left a further sum of fifty thousand dollars for the purpose of erecting model lodging houses, the income of the rents to be forever applied to certain public charities. He received, in 1854, the honorary degree of Doctor of Laws from Harvard College, and also from that of Williamstown.

Viewing his character phrenologically, it was the symmetry and beauty of the whole organization which constituted its excellence, without the peculiar prominence or exaggeration of particular organs which give the highest power of genius in their manifestation. In other words, his intellectual and moral powers were in due and admirable proportion—with no deficiency and with no excess. In his person, he was at the same time commanding and prepossessing, with a suavity and air of benevolence and sincerity which indicated the perfect gentleman.

In his social relations he was eminently happy. Early in life, he married Catherine, the daughter of the Hon. Timothy Bigelow, long known and distinguished as the Speaker of the House of Representatives of Massachusetts. She aided in his labors with devoted fidelity, and shared in his honors with becoming dignity. He lived to see a numerous family of children well married, and settled in life. His eldest son married the daughter of the eminent historian Prescott.

In June, 1855, he was attacked with alarming symptoms of disease. These continued to increase, and his life was brought to a close on the 18th day of August, in the sixty-third year of his age. He was, in principle and practice, during life, a sincere and pious Christian. He met death as becomes a Christian to die. At this comparatively early age, with everything about him calculated to make the close of life a period of calm and tranquil enjoyment, in the consciousness of a life well spent, he resigned his spirit to the God who gave it, without a murmur or expression of anything but gratitude for the blessings he had experienced.

There was no circumstance of his life more remarkable than the demonstration of public feeling during his sickness, and after his death. During the last few lingering days of his life, there seemed to be but one topic on the public mind. Was there any hope? Is he to die? Seldom has the death of an individual, holding no public office, called forth such an expression of deep feeling. Faneuil Hall, on a short notice, was spontaneously crowded by our citizens, in order to give vent to their grief. Speeches were made by several of our most distinguished men. It was the loss of a friend, of a general benefactor, of a good man, which called forth this universal expression of sorrow. The government of Harvard College, and a great number of Societies held special meetings, and adopted resolutions to attend his funeral. The Rev.

Dr. Lothrop, his pastor, in a funeral discourse did justice to his religious character. He says, "The benevolence of Mr. Lawrence, and all the virtues of his life, had their strong foundation and constant nourishment in religious faith. He believed in his heart, on the Lord Jesus Christ, and received him as the promised Messiah and Saviour of the World. He was truly catholic in his feelings, loving all who love our Lord Jesus Christ in sincerity and truth; and extended the helping hand of his charities to the enterprises of various Christian denominations."

Mr. Lawrence's connection with our own Society was brief, his election having taken place in December, 1853; but he entered deeply into the spirit of our pursuits, and contemplated making some valuable contributions to our archives. His name will be always cherished as one of the most distinguished upon our rolls.

Printed by Libri Plureos GmbH in Hamburg, Germany